UNLOAD YOUR OWN DONKEY

Primrose Arnander **Ashkhain Skipwith**

with illustrations by
Kathryn Lamb

STACEY INTERNATIONAL

UNLOAD YOUR OWN DONKEY

Published by Stacey International
128 Kensington Church Street
London W8 4BH
Tel: 020 7221 7166; Fax: 020 7792 9288
Email: info@stacey-international.co.uk

Reprinted 2007

ISBN 9781900988360
2 4 6 8 0 9 7 5 3

British Library Cataloguing-in-Publication Data
A catalogue record for this publication is available from the British Library

Printed and bound in Singapore by Tien Wah Press

Note on transliteration

The form of transliteration used is one that has been developed over recent years, somewhat simplified in the hope it will help those with little or no Arabic to articulate the proverbs in their original language. Most of the transliterations are self-evident, but a few comments may be useful.

ẓ ṭ ḍ ṣ ḥ	are hard letters, heavily pronounced
dh th	equivalent to th (as in there and think, respectively)
ā ū ī	are long (as in baa, moon, seen)
kh	equivalent to ch, as in loch
gh	rolled, as in the French letter r
q	represents the Arabic qaaf (hard k)
'	before and after letters, represents the Arabic letters ayn and hamza, which have no English equivalent. The exact sound cannot be explained easily in writing, the nearest equivalent being a glottal stop or hesitation.

Authors' Preface

We are delighted to present our third collection of Arab proverbs and sayings – a sequel to *The Son of a Duck is a Floater* and *Apricots Tomorrow*. We are grateful to the many people who encouraged us to compile a third book and suggested proverbs for inclusion.

As with the previous two titles, the proverbs for this edition come from all over the Arab world, but while the vocabulary may vary from country to country (Egyptian readers have remarked that they would say 'the son of a *goose* is a floater'), the underlying meaning remains the same.

The same format prevails; the Arabic proverb is followed by its transliteration, a literal translation and the English equivalent, sometimes embellished by a quotation or comment.

Kathryn Lamb – now herself the author and illustrator of eight books about childhood and growing up – has once again provided the delightful illustrations which are such an integral part of the series.

We hope that this collection of proverbs will, like its predecessors, amuse and entertain, and perhaps cause the reader to ponder the common heritage of humour and wisdom of both the East and the West.

Primrose Arnander **Ashkhain Skipwith**

Introduction

Travelling through Arabia a while ago for several weeks on end, I was struck by the frequency with which my Arab companion's funnybone was tickled by just those things which tickled mine. Back at *beit* Arnander in Jeddah, I remarked on this to my hostess, Primrose. She responded by opening up a drawer of her desk to reveal the Arabic proverbs and adages she and Ashkhain Skipwith had been carefully researching to illustrate how precisely the wisdom and wit of one culture reflected the other's. There before us was the draft of *The Son of a Duck is a Floater.* So enthusiastically did Arabic and English speakers alike take to that little book that *Apricots Tomorrow* swiftly followed – to the same welcome. Now the authors offer a third garnering of traditional Arabic saws to delight the aficionados of cross-cultural unity, where horse sense provokes a horse laugh in two languages.

Tom Stacey

صار للذبابة دكّانة وبتسَكِّر على بَكّير

Ṣār lidhubāba dukkāna wa bitsakkir 'alā bakkīr

The fly has acquired a shop and it is closing early

The fly is out of his depth

دكان
CLOSED
مقفل
WATER
WA
HONEY
LABAN
EMPTY

الـدَّيْـن هَـمّ في الليل وذلّ في النهار

Aldayn hamm billayl, wa dhul finnahār

Debt is a worry in the night and a misery in the day

He that goes a-borrowing goes a-sorrowing

خُـد الأصيلة ونام على حصيرة

Khud alaṣīla wanām 'alā ḥaṣīra

Marry the woman of good background even if you have to sleep on a mat

Better a fortune in a wife than with a wife

إذا كان فيه خير ما كانش رماه الطير

Idhā kān fīh khayr mā kansh ramā aṭṭayr

If there were any good in it the bird would not have dropped it

There's no mileage in it

زي السمن والعسل

Zay alsamn wal'asal

Like butter and honey

Love and marriage go together like a horse and carriage

Sammy Cahn, from the musical *Our Town*

خفّ أحمالها تطول أعمارها

Khif aḥmālhā titawwil a'mārhā

Lighten their burden, lengthen their lives

Use the carrot rather than the stick

خلِّي الزيت في أجـراره، لمن تيجي أسـعاره

Khallī azzayt fī ajraru, lamman tījī as'āru

Keep oil in its containers until the price is right

Keep your powder dry

ذاب ذوبة الملح

Dhāb dhawbat almilḥ

Dissolved like salt

Melted into thin air

لا تعشق الغرباء فهم على رحيل

Lā ta'shaq alghurabā' fahum 'alā raḥīl

Don't fall in love with strangers, they are on a journey

Ships that pass in the night

الأقارب مثل العقارب

Alaqarib mithl al 'aqāarib

Relatives are like scorpions

Many kinsfolk, few friends

ثلاثة ما بينْعارو ،الفرد والفرس والمرأة

Thalātha mā biyin'ārū, alfard, walfaras, walmar'a

Three things are not lendable: the rifle, the horse and the woman

A horse, a wife and a sword may be shown but not lent

بيطلع الضَّو بدون صياح الدِّيك

Biyiṭla' aḍḍaw bidūn ṣiyāḥ addīk

Dawn breaks without the crowing of the cock

Time and tide wait for no man

يا مأمِّـنَـة على الرجال مأمِّـنَـة للميّـة في الغربال

Yā muammina 'alā arrijāl, muammina lilmaya filghurbāl

You who trust in men entrust the water to the sieve

Love is eternal while it lasts

"Trust none. For oaths are straws, men's faiths are wafer-cakes."
(*Henry V* – William Shakespeare)

إيش ماطبخت الرعنا بياكل جوزها الأَعمى

Aysh mā ṭabakhat arra'nā biyākul jawzhā ala'mā

Whatever the crazy wife cooks her blind husband will eat

She gets away with murder

الإبريق المليان مايلقلقش

Alibrīq almalyān mā yīlaqlaqsh

Water does not slosh in a full water jug

Steady as a rock

A person with bottom

من قلل عقله تعبت رجليه

Man qallal 'aqlu ti'bat rijlayh

The small of brain tires his feet

Use your head and save your legs

إبنه على كتـفه ويدوّر عليـه

Ibnu 'alā kitfu wa yidawwir 'alayh

His son is on his shoulder, and he is searching for him

He can't see for looking

البيضة مين باضها والدجاجة مين جابها

Albayḍa mīn bāḍhā waddajāja mīn jabhā

The egg, who laid it? The chicken, who delivered it?

Which came first – the chicken or the egg?

فصِّل وإحنا بنلبس

Faṣṣil wa iḥnā binilbis

You cut and we will wear

The ball is in your court

ما كل من ركب الحصان خيَّال

Mā kul man rikib alḥuṣān khayyāl

Not everyone who has ridden a horse is a horseman

A hammer does not a blacksmith make

اللي بيخلط حاله مع النخالة بتاكله الدجاج

Illī biyikhluṭ ḥālu ma' alnakhāla bitāklu addajāj

He who mixes himself with bran will be eaten by the chickens

A man is judged by the company he keeps

من حلَّ حزامه بات

Man ḥalla ḥizāmu bāt

He who unties his belt will stay the night

Actions speak louder than words

المعزة العياطة ما ياكلش إبنها الديب

Almi'za al'ayyāṭa mā yākulsh ibnahā addīib

The bleating goat will not have her son eaten by the wolf

The more you claim, the more you gain

ما ينفعك إلا عجل بقرتك

Mā yinfa 'ak illā 'ijl baqaratak

Nothing will do you any good except the calf of your own cow

Paddle your own canoe

الإيد التعبانة شبعانة

Al īd alta'bāna shab'āna

A tired hand is a satisfied hand

No pain, no gain

النقطة الدايمة بتبجش الحجر

Annaqṭa addayma bitibkhish al ḥajar

Continuous dripping wears away the stone

A proverb shared by both languages

Much rain wears the marble
(*Henry VI* – William Shakespeare)

إشتهينا الدجاجة أكلناها بريشها

Ishtahaynā addajāja akalnāhā birīshhā

We so desired the chicken we ate it with its feathers

We ate ourselves silly

أخرس عاقل أفضل من جاهل ناطق

Akhras 'āqil afḍal min jāhil nāṭiq

An intelligent mute rather than an ignorant talker

Better to remain silent and be thought a fool than to speak out and remove all doubt.
(Abraham Lincoln – *Golden Book)*

لابس الخلاخل و البلاء من الداخل

Lābis alkhalākhil walbalā min addakhil

Wearring jingling bracelets but rotten from within

Poison is poison though it comes in a golden cup

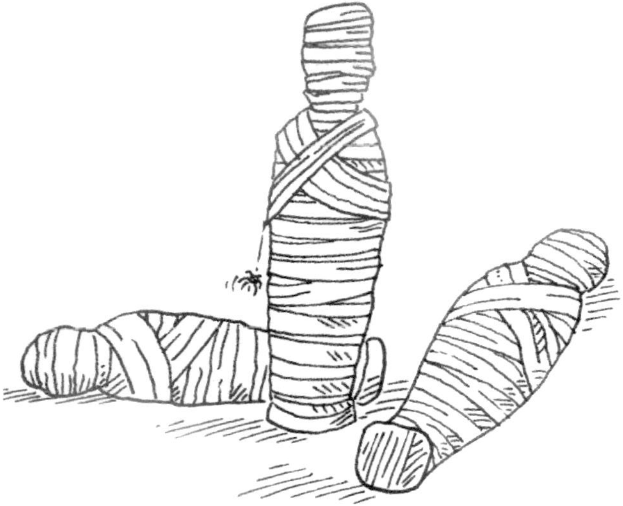

الكَفَن مالوش جيوب

Alkafan mālush juyūb

The shroud has no pockets

A proverb shared by both languages

You can't take it with you!

قالوا للبغل أبوك مين ،قال الفرس خالي

*Qālū lilbaghl abūk mīn, qāl alfaras khālī**

They said to the mule, "Who is your father?" He said, "The horse is my uncle."

Everyone is kin to the rich man

"Lloyd George knew my father, father knew Lloyd George."
(Popular 1920s song referring to the British Prime Minister)

*The Arabic word *khāl* refers to the maternal uncle; '*amm* is the word for paternal uncle.
A mule is the offspring of a donkey and a mare, but prefers to gloss over his weaker paternal lineage.

إمسك الحبل يدلك على الوتد

Imsik alḥabl yidillak 'alā alwatad

Hold on to the rope, it will lead you to the stake

Follow the river and you'll get to the sea

زي البصل محشور في كل طعام

Zayy albaṣal maḥshūr fī kull ṭa'ām

Like onion it arrives in every dish

A finger in every pie

اللي تطبل له يرقص

Illī tiṭabbil lū yurquṣ

Whatever you play for him on the drums, he will dance to

He will dance to your tune

يا نحلة لا تقرصيني ولا عايز مِنّك عسل

Yā naḥla lā tuqruṣīnī walā 'āyiz minnik 'asal

Oh bee, don't sting me and I don't want your honey

Discretion is the better part of valour

زي دُود المش منه فيه

Zayy dūd almish minnu fīh

As the worm is in the cheese, so it is of the cheese

Sufficient unto the day is the evil thereof

(Matthew 6:34)

اللي إتلسع من الشربة بينفخ في الزبادي

Illī itlisa' min ashshurba biyunfukh fizzabādī

He who has been scalded by soup, blows on yoghurt

Once bitten, twice shy

الصِّيت و لا الغنى

Aṣṣayt walā alghinā

Good reputation rather than wealth

A good name is worth more than riches

لا بقر ولا منغدي على سحر

Lā baqar walā minghaddī 'alā saḥar

No cows, no feeding them at dawn

Every cloud has a silver lining

العقربة أخت الحية

Al'aqraba ukht alḥayya

The scorpion is the snake's sister

Tarred with the same brush

كلٌ يغني على ليلاه

Kullun yughannī 'alā laylāh

Each one sings of his Laila

Every Romeo has his Juliet

Majnoon Laila (Crazy for Laila) is a classic Arab love story

ركبته ورايا حط إيده في الخرج

Rakkabtu warāyā ḥaṭṭ īdu filkhurj

I set him behind me, he put his hand in the saddlebag

To nurse a viper in the bosom

صباح الفوّال و لا صباح العطّار

Ṣabāḥ alfawwāl walā ṣabāḥ al'aṭṭār

At early morn it is better to meet the seller of ful than the seller of perfume

There is a time and a place for everything

(*Ful* is a breakfast dish of broad beans)

كل شارب له مقص

Kull shārib lū miquṣṣ

Every moustache has its scissors

Horses for courses

عاوز الحق ولا إبن عمه

'āwiz alhaqq wāllā ibn 'ammu

Do you want justice or its cousin

The good is the enemy of the best

تخربش القط يخربشك

Tikharbish alqiṭṭ yikharbishak

You scratch the cat and it will scratch you

To give as good as you get

اللي بده يعمل جَّمال لازم يعلي باب داره

Illī biddu yi'mal jammāl lāzim yi'allī bāb dāru

He who wants to be a camel driver must raise the door of his house

Put your money where your mouth is

الكلام زي حبل الصوف ،كل ما تشده بيتمط

Alkalām zay ḥabl aṣṣūf, kull mā tishiddu biyitmaṭṭ

Talk is like a woollen rope; you pull it, it stretches

To spin a yarn

نواية تسند الجرة

Nawaya tisnid aljarra

A tiny date stone can steady the water jar

Great matters turn on a little pin

ولد السكافي حافي

Walad alsakkāfī ḥāfī

The son of the cobbler goes barefoot

A proverb shared by both languages

زَوِّج ابنك متى أردت و ابنتك متى قدرت

Zawwij ibnak matā aradta wa ibnatak matā qadarta

Marry your son when you want and your daughter when you can

A proverb shared by both languages

جارك القريب ولا أخوك البعيد

Jārak alqarīb walā akhūk alba'īd

Rather the neighbour who is near than your brother who is far

A near neighbour is better than a far kinsman

لمّا أنا ست و أنتي ست مين يكب الطشت

Lammā anā sitt wa intī sitt mīn yikubb aṭṭisht

If I am a lady and you are a lady who will empty the chatty

The pecking order has yet to be established

قافلة فايتة ولا حمار مربوط

Qāfila fāyta walā ḥimār marbūt

Rather a passing caravan than a tethered donkey

It is better to travel hopefully than to arrive

DONKEY
FOOD
DONKEY
FOOD

إذا لم تكن منارة فكن على الأقل شمعة

Idhā lam takun manāra fakun 'alā alaqall sham'a

If you cannot be a lighthouse, at least be a candle

Not every light is the sun

النمل بيظهر من مطبخه جوعان

Annaml biyidhhar min maṭbakhu ju'ān

The ants leave his kitchen hungry

As mean as Scrooge
(Charles Dickens' famous miser)

مثل الدجاج ،مابيهدس إلا بالغربلة

Mithl addajāj, ma biyihdis ilā bilgharbala

Like chickens they think only of what falls from the sieve

To look no further than the end of your nose

زي العسل على القشطة

Zay al'asal 'alā alqishṭa

Like honey on top of cream

The gilt on the gingerbread

الجاهل بيتعلم من كيسه ،والعاقل من كيس غيره

Aljāhil biyit'allam min kīsu, wal'āqil min kīs ghayru

The ignorant learns at his own expense and the wise at the expense of others

Wise men learn from other men's mistakes, fools from their own

اصبر على الحصرم تاكله عنب

Uṣbur 'alā alḥuṣrum tāklu 'inab

Be patient through the verjuice, you will eat grapes

Everything comes to him who waits

بيت الكريم عنده زبالة كثيرة

Bayt alkarīm 'indu zibāla kathīra

The house of the generous piles high the rubbish

Every picture tells a story

Lavish cooking leads to full dustbins

أنا غني و بحب الهديّة

Anā ghanī wabaḥibb alhadiyya

I am rich yet like gifts

Enough is good, but a feast is better

In contrast to: *Enough is as good as a feast*

إذا كان راسك من شمع فلا تمشي في الشمس

Idhā kān rāsak min shami' falā tamshī fishshams

If your head is made of wax do not walk in the sun

If you can't stand the heat, get out of the kitchen

نزِّل عن جحشك

Nazzil 'an jaḥshak

Unload your own donkey

Mind your own business

زيتنا في دقيقنا

Zaytnā fī daqīqnā

Our oil is in our flour

Everything in the garden is rosy

بنت الفارة حفارة

Bint alfāra ḥaffāra

The daughter of a mouse is a digger

A chip off the old block

قرد يحبك ولا غزال يمقتك

Qird yiḥubbak walā ghazāl yimqutak

Rather be loved by a monkey than despised by a gazelle

Take what you can get

بعد أمي و أختي الباقي كله جيران

Ba'd ummī wa ukhtī, albāqī kullu jīrān

After my mother and my sister, the rest are all neighbours

Blood is thicker than water

النار ولا العار

Annār walā al'ār

Rather be touched by fire than by dishonour

Take away my good name and you take away my life

اللي طلّع الحمار عالسطح ينزّله

Illī ṭalla' alḥimār 'assaṭḥ yinazzilu

Whoever took the donkey up to the roof should bring it down

You got us into this mess; now get us out of it

يا رايح عالجبل جيب معاك ولو حجر

Yā rayiḥ 'aljabal jīb ma'āk walaw ḥajar

You who are going to the mountain bring something back, even if it is a stone

Don't forget the souvenir!

إعمل الخير وارميه في البحر

I'mal alkhayr wa irmīh filbaḥr

Do good and throw it in the sea

Virtue is its own reward

"The greatest pleasure I know is to do good by stealth."
(*Athenaeum* – Charles Lamb)

كل واحد له بذنجان شكل

Kull wāḥid lu badhinjān shikl

Everyone favours a different eggplant

There is no accounting for tastes

الأكل في الشبعان خسـارة

Al akl fi ashshab'ān khisāra

Food for the well-fed is a waste

Preaching to the converted

ما كل جني يدخل القـنيـنة

Mā kul jinnī yadkhul alqannīna

Not every genie re-enters the bottle

You can't turn the clock back

من غاب غاب نصيـبه

Man ghāb ghāb naṣību

He who is absent loses his share

The absent saint gets no candle

الأحمق ينصح في الوقت الدَّيِق

Alaḥmaq yinṣaḥ fi alwaqt aldayyiq

The idiot gives advice in tight corners

"Fools rush in where angels fear to tread"
(*An Essay on Criticism* – Alexander Pope)

أكلوا الهدية وكسروا الزبدية

Akalū alhadiyya wakasarū alzibdiyya

They ate the gift and broke the container

Small gifts make friends, great ones make enemies

اللي يعمل جميل يتمه

Illī yi'mal jamīl yitimmu

He who does a favour completes it

Good to begin well, better to end well

المستعجل والبطيء عند المعدية يلتقي

Almusta'jil walbaṭī' 'ind almu'addiya yiltaqī

The speedy and the slow meet at the ferry

Slow and steady wins the race

مش كل أسود فحمة ومش كل أبيض شحمة

Mish kull aswad faḥma, wa mish kull abyaḍ shaḥma

Not everything black is a piece of charcoal, and not everything white is tallow

All that glisters is not gold
(*The Merchant of Venice* – William Shakespeare)

شرط في الحقلة ولا قتال عالبيدر

Sharṭ filḥaqla wala qitāl 'albaydar

Strike the deal in the field rather than dispute on the threshing floor

Forewarned is forearmed

لو البومة فيها خير ما فاتها الصياد

Law albūma fīhā khayr mā fāthā aṣṣayād

Had there been any good in the owl, the hunter would not have passed it by

The game is not worth the candle

الفلوس زَي العصافير تروح وتيجي

Alfulūs zayy al'aṣāfīr tirūḥ watījī

Money is like birds, it comes and goes

Money is round and rolls away

Harrods
BOUTIQUE TRÈS CHIC (ET CHÈRE)
100

من يزرع الشوك لا يحصد العنب

Man yazra' ashshawk lā yaḥṣid al'inab

He who sows the thorn does not reap the grapes

Garbage in, garbage out

طنجرة لقت غطاها

Ṭanjara laqat ghaṭāhā

The saucepan has found its lid

To every Jack his Jill

قوة الصوت لو بتنفع كان الحمار ابتـنى العلالي

Quwwat alṣawt law bitinfa' kān alḥimār ibtanā al'alālī

If a loud voice were of any use a donkey would have built high castles

Fine words butter no parsnips

الجنة بدون ناس ما بتنداس

Aljanna bidūn nās mā bitindās

Paradise without people is not worth stepping into

A soul alone neither sings nor weeps

لا شفت الجمل ولا الجمّال

Lā shuft aljamal walā aljammāl

I have seen neither the camel nor the camel rider

I've seen neither hide nor hair of them

ياكل التمر و يرجم بالنوى

Yākul attamir wayarjum binnawā

He eats the dates and attacks with the stones

He bites the hand that feeds him

ما كل معوج الرقبة جمل

Mā kul mu'awwaj arraqaba jamal

Not everything with a crooked neck is a camel

It's not the beard that makes the philosopher

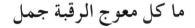

الرّايب ما يرجعش حليب

Arrayib mā yirja'sh ḥalīb

Buttermilk does not turn back into milk

You can't unscramble the omelette

التاجر المفلس يدور على الدفاتر القديمة

Altājir almuflis yidawwir 'ala addafātir al qadīma

The bankrupt merchant searches the old books

Flogging a dead horse

هربنا من الدب وقعنا في الجب

Harabnā min addib waqa'nā fi aljibb

We escaped from the bear and fell into the trap

Out of the frying pan into the fire

إنصح جاهل يعاديك

Inṣaḥ jāhil yi'ādīk

Advise the ignorant and become his enemy

Give neither counsel nor salt till you are asked for it

بيفصِّل للبرغوث قميص

Bifaṣṣil lilbarghūth qamīṣ

He cuts a shirt for the flea

He is a nit picker

لولا الكاسورة ماكانت الفاخورة

Law lā alkāsūra mā kānat alfākhūra

If it were not for breakages, there would be no potters

It's an ill wind that blows nobody any good

اللي بده ياكل عسل بيصبر على قرص النحل

Illī biddu yākul 'asal biyuṣbur 'alā qarṣ alnaḥl

He who wants to eat honey will bear the sting of the bees

Honey is sweet, but the bee stings

RUPERT
BROOKE
LABAN
HONEY

مقدمة من المؤلفتيْن

انه لمن دواعي سرورنا أن نقدّم مجموعتنا الثالثة للأقوال والأمثال العربية ـ تكملة لسابقتيها، إبن البط عوّام، وبكره في المشمش.. ونتوجه بالشكر والامتنان للكثيرين الذين شجعونا على تجميع موادّ الكتاب الثالث وزوّدونا بالأمثال العديدة.
وكما كان الحال في الكتابين السابقين فإن الأمثال الواردة في هذا الكتاب يعود مصدرها الى جميع أنحاء العالم العربي.
وربما تختلف بعض مفردات الكلمات من قطر لآخر فالمصريون مثلاً يقولون إبن (الوزّ عوّام) إلا أن المقصود من المعنى يظلّ على حاله. كما أن الشكل يحافظ على نفسه، ويتبع المثل العربي ترجمة حرفية له وما يقابله باللغة الانجليزية مع تذويقه بتعليق او اقتباس في بعض الأحيان.
لقد قدّمت كاثرين لامب ـ التي انجزت حتى الآن تأليف ثمانية كتب عن تربية الأطفال وهي نفسها أم لستة أطفال ـ هذه الكتب ومرة أخرى زينتها برسومها الجميلة التي تشكل جزءاً لا يتجزأ من هذه السلسلة .
نأمل ان تكون هذه المجموعة من الأمثال كسابقاتها ممتعة ومسلّية، وربما تجعل القارىء يتأمل في التراث المشترك في الفكاهة والحكمة ما بين الشرق والغرب.

بريمروز آرناندر　　　　أشخين سكيبويث

مقدمة

قبل فترة وجيزة جبت أنحاء الجزيرة العربية على مدى أسابيع عدة، ودهشت لتكرار ما أثار حس الدعابة لدى صاحبي العربي كما أثاره لدي. فإذا ما عدت إلى بيت أرناندر في جدة، أبلغت مضيفتي برمروز بملاحظتي. وقد ردت بأن فتحت درج مكتبها وأخرجت منه الأمثلة والأقوال العربية المأثورة التي عكفت هي واشخين سكيبويث على بحثها بأناة بغية إظهار كيف أن حكمة وفطنة ثقافة ما تعكس بتطابق ودقة حكمة وفطنة ثقافة أخرى. ولم يكن ما عرضته علي سوى مسودة كتاب 'فرخ البط عوام' (ذ صن أوف اى داك ايز اى فلوتر). وهو الكتاب الصغير الذي كان إقبال الناطقين بالعربية والإنكليزية عليه كبيراً جداً إلى درجة أن كتاب 'بالمشمش' (آبريكوتس تومورو) صدر بسرعة بعده ليلقى استقبالاً لا يقل حماسة في الأوساط. والآن، يخرج علينا المؤلفون بمجموعة ثالثة من الأقوال العربية المأثورة يطرب لها المهتمون بما يجمع بين مختلف الثقافات، حيث نشاهد كيف أن المنطق السليم في لغة قادر على أن يثير الإحساس كل الإحساس في لغة أخرى.

توم ستيسي

Published by
Stacey International
128 Kensington Church Street
London W8 4BH
Tel: 020 7221 7166; Fax: 020 7792 9288
E-mail: stacey-inter@btconnect.com

ISBN 1 900988 364

قسم معلومات تصنيف المنشورات في المكتبة
البريطانية يمكن الحصول على سجل تصنيفي
لهذا الكتاب من المكتبة البريطانية.

تمت طباعة وتجليد هذا الكتاب في مطبعة
تيان واه للنشر - سنغافورة

نزِّل عن جحشك

بريمروز آرناندر   اشخين سكيبويث

الصور بريشة
كاثرين لامب

من اعداد مجمعو «إبن البط عوام» و «بكرة في المشمش»